Graceline

This
th

Jane Duran

Graceline

ENITHARMON PRESS

First published in 2010
by Enitharmon Press
26B Caversham Road
London NW5 2DU

www.enitharmon.co.uk

Distributed in the UK by
Central Books
99 Wallis Road
London E9 5LN

Distributed in the USA and Canada
by Dufour Editions Inc.
PO Box 7, Chester Springs
PA 19425, USA

ISBN: 978-1-904634-99-7

Enitharmon Press gratefully acknowledges the financial support of
Arts Council England, London.

British Library Cataloguing-in-Publication Data.
A catalogue record for this book is available
from the British Library.

Typeset in Albertina by Libanus Press
and printed in England by
Antony Rowe Ltd

ACKNOWLEDGEMENTS

Poems, or versions of poems, from this collection have appeared in the *Long Poem Magazine, Magma, Poetry London, Poetry Review*, and in the anthology *Contourlines* (Salt Publishing with Magdalene College Publications, 2009).

I am indebted to Mimi Khalvati, Sue MacIntyre, Sofía Prats, Marisol Téllez and my sister Cheli Durán for reading the manuscript and commenting with such care; to Moniza Alvi for her thoughtful suggestions when this sequence was beginning to take shape; to Robert McNab whose book *Ghost Ships* suggested a pathway for this one. Matthew Parker's history *Panama Fever* was a rich source of information and insight for my poem 'Panama Canal'. I am grateful to John Emery, Shafeek Fazal and Don Hazeldine who helped me to access information on the Grace Line ships.

My warm thanks to Susy Andai and Guillermo García Huidobro for their hospitality and guidance in Chile, and to Diana Meredith and Carol Meredith for our shared journey in the south. Warm thanks also to Stephen Stuart-Smith and Isabel Brittain at Enitharmon Press for their encouragement, patience and painstaking editorial work.

AUTHOR'S NOTE

In the autumn of 1955 I travelled with my mother and sisters on a Grace Line ship, the *Santa Barbara*, from New York City to Valparaíso, Chile. My father had been posted to Santiago with the United Nations Economic Commission for Latin America (*CEPAL*) and was awaiting our arrival. The *Santa Barbara* was one of the 'combo' ships in the Grace Line fleet, a small ship carrying both cargo and passengers. It passed from the Atlantic to the Pacific through the Panama Canal, and then travelled down the west coast of Latin America, stopping at many ports. This long, and to me mysterious transition between cultures and landscapes has been a point of departure and return for these poems.

Among the passengers on board was Major Carlos Prats, who was returning home after studying in the United States. Many years later Carlos Prats became Commander-in-Chief of the Army, and in 1972 Minister of Internal Affairs and Vice President of Chile in Allende's government. He went into exile in Argentina after Pinochet's coup. He and his wife Sofía Cuthbert were assassinated in Buenos Aires in 1974. My sequence *Invisible Ink* is dedicated to their daughter, my friend Sofía.

for my sisters Cheli and Lucy

Caminante, no hay camino,
sino estelas en la mar.

Traveller, there is no road,
only wakes in the sea.

Antonio Machado

CONTENTS

INVISIBLE INK

INVISIBLE INK

MORPHOLOGY

Let's just say there are disguises, layers,
        that one landscape can seem
to lie in another, in wait, or change aspect

overnight. A landscape withheld for the moment,
        or holding, like a new person in the old.
So I look up and there it is again –

the mountain that still measures my progress
        as I walk slowly by.
It is a sort of grandfather clock

the sun catches in a room.
        It has the feel of a long summer
that no one imagines will ever end

and uncanny resemblances to friends,
        to people I love, these harshest of slopes.
As if it knows already what I am becoming,

what I will choose to be. And then its face
        changes, the expression softens.

GRID

A child's notebook, faint red
and purple lines crossed by turquoise lines,
pages of tiny squares – a discipline.

The cover is marbled, aquamarine,
and the shopkeeper tired and kind
among the dusty papers.

A mother and child cross the plaza
in the shop window, against the wind.
My notebook is stapled hastily

so the papers won't come free,
won't blow away when I am out on deck
passing countries I can't even see.

I will take this starting point.
Any of these squares will do.

*

The *Santa Barbara* leaves New York harbour
for Valparaíso. Our journey away
is so gradual, the city now

a festive goodbye. My feelings today
are keepsakes of this square.
Then they spill out, they begin to enter

all the elsewheres in the notebook.

*

Will the rain interrupt my thoughts
or is it too silent, falling into itself
as it strikes the sea?

None of the dawns I have known
open so abruptly as here.
The hoops of my earrings tremble
before so much life.

*

Every day we are somewhere new
along the grid.
I am so beautifully contained here,

as if nothing bad could ever happen to me.
Yet whenever I want
I can travel to the next square

and the next, along a curve,
always knowing just where I am
and where I have been

in a summation of squares:
West 16th Street, Cristóbal,
Buenaventura, Salaverry,

Callao, Arica, Antofagasta.
Chañaral, Valparaíso.
There is make-believe and reality in it,

pleats oil makes on water.
Yet the true sea is here alongside me,
all one – a state of grace,

where any grid fades
or burns off in a mist.

*

On the last day
I sit by a woman
with yellow, pink and green scarves

wrapped round her head
and tied at the nape of her neck.
The grey hairs she has not captured
catch the evening light on deck.

She hums to herself
and her arms have wounds
where she scratches.
She rubs her upper arms, her hands,

so the mother of pearl bracelets
and the reddened seed-bracelets
almost slip off. Her skin shifts
over her bones. There is a flaw

in the china cup she drinks from,
a *y* cut in the rim. The sea is shallow
now, a tremulous, perpetual line.

I touch her hand.
I ask her to sing for me
and she begins.

CANVAS

Somehow all my thoughts
        still pass through this screen,
                the one embroidered   with birds,

uncertainties,   torrential rains,
        butterflies.

How slow the ship is,
        how earnest each of our days
           on board

as if there was something intricate
           to be understood
                before we can arrive anywhere.

Even the seagulls that come near us
        as we catch the eye of land

           know no restraint. *Where were you?* they seem to say,
        threading,

or *At last* –
           over each measured
and illusory homecoming.

GRACELINE
after The Sea *by Max Ernst*

I still see the wake of our ship,
    or the route our ship took
        combed evenly across the ocean.

It makes graceful lines
    that have a way of lasting:
        so spontaneous and definite

I could start our journey all over again
    and live in the present.
        In his painting of the sea,

that comb – a few teeth missing –
    scraped away the recent white
        and oatmeal oils

to show at last the older blues and blacks:
    this makes a restless
        pattern over the sea

the way a ship performs just this task, with fidelity,
    to scratch what is already there
        with a little incident, remark, anecdote –

a grazed knee, a few shouts in a port,
    so for the passengers on deck,
        the ocean becomes theirs,

dense and dependable, even homely.
    They leave what can never be left.
        The ship creates the illusion of a path –

a past that issues from it and winds
    over the ocean and is unforgettable,
        and the ocean is unforgettable.

CHIMERAS

What if the ship were put together
       with safety pins, newspaper,
cotton, paste and sawdust?

Or what if there was nothing to it?
       What if the deck never happened,
the ochres and reds I remember

giving the lie, and at night
       no beguiling surfaces, railings, rain?

And what if that port, the one that was
       or might have been –

the open promenade, laughter,
       palm trees, crates of coffee, papayas,
the sky almost a royal blue,

were just my love telling tales,
       being there, colouring in
all the lavish and lost places?

BOATLAND

There are times when the boat stirs
    laterally, as if with its last
        reserves of strength,

and oil glistens below,
    and there are still no sheep,
        no hillsides of rain alongside us –

rain on them so light
    it is almost dew,
        no owls or goldfinches,

forests, none at all. But the cargo,
    the convincing heaviness of the boat
        suggest land all the time – after all

my feet touch wood whenever I want,
    the intermittent creakings something divined,
        imagined, not quite long

or real enough to take seriously,
    those wet ports, buttresses that give way,
        waves that enter the porous docks,

land splashing out eagerly towards me.

TONNAGE

As soon as I saw it in Lloyd's Register of Shipping –
the *Santa Barbara*, I saw its official number: 249411,
and its gross tonnage, 8357, the deadweight
tonnage at the summer load line 9764.
Its port of registry was New York, builders
the North Carolina Shipbuilding Company,
year 1946. It had 3 decks, and 2 steam turbines
double reduction geared to screw shaft –
built in Lynn by the General Electric Company.
The breadth extreme of the hull was 63 feet
and 2 inches. 2 inches! The tall, courteous librarian
at the Guildhall Library said his own garden
was 60 feet long, so he stepped back and showed me
how broad our ship might have been – from where
to where in the Reading Room, that is –
from near the printers and photocopier as far as
the panelling and computers at the back,
which was not far. And I imagined the *Santa Barbara*,
her decks, the long wooden tables and heavy registers,
leatherbound Voyage Supplements – yellow and fraying,
the padding and hesitant footsteps of the readers –
and our ship rose with a shout from its waves
and the water fell off it like streamers.

CONCEALMENT

One side of the ship is cast in sunlight.
      The ship that passes the mountain.
      The mountain that passes the ship.

My friend Pearl is at the dock
      in Panama City. She waves to us
      and smiles, the way her mother waves

and smiles. When we see their faces from the deck
      there is a moment of joy and recognition
      and homecoming. Did they pass us by

or we them? We don't see them anymore.
      And grief is to be expected too,
      one weather dragged by the hand,

combed by my fingers
      all the way into another
      where I know little or nothing

          and ask questions constantly.

PANAMA CANAL

En mi soledad
he visto cosas muy claras,
que no son verdad.

In my solitude/I have seen things very clearly/that are not true.

Antonio Machado

1

Unerringly, our ship recovers speed.
        There is a splinter in my foot
my mother takes out with a needle.

Seeing each port for the first time
        I cannot immediately interpret it.
I hold the picture upside down, I squint,

and there is also what happens to land
        faraway, as the weather changes,
and to language in all its emotive climates.

The ship dreams a little
        as it waits in the Gatún Lock.
I feel the tumult of its patience under my feet.

2

Now liners pass us on the Canal,
        swanky cruisers showing off,
cargo ships with red or black funnels,

nothing helpless or impeded.
        On deck my sister holds her hands out –
the butterflies travel against us

or round us, blue and haphazard,
        a mild resistance.
The locks open for us, along the banks

gauzy smalltown-America streets pursue us,
 and a jungle passes through our ship.

3

The men digging on the slopes,
 exhausted or sick, stop to look up.
Soft colours in the sepia photograph

are washed in by computer,
 artifice – the pale blues
and rust of their shirts, their trousers;

only the sober eyes are dark
 (for who was smiling?) like level tides
with nowhere to go.

4

Colón, bar-town at the hard
 edge of water, Bottle Alley,

men leaning on the bar doors
 out of the sun,

in the alcohol-soaked mud street:
 a day that came and went

but lingered a little
 before it left finally, had in it

a letter, a letter from
 somewhere else

with no terror, no yellow fever,
 no sliding mud, broken boots

and in her handwriting –
        dry, dry – an open door

to a smallholding.

5

I think of a mud street filling up
        with empty bottles.
A man walks over them,

the perilous bridge they make.
        I think of the rum
he pours down his throat,

hat over his eyes
        and how it feels good to be
where he is for a few minutes,

to be in that heat after a downpour
        where the malaria
and yellow fever mosquitoes

can drink from him
        away from the workers' camp,
seventy men to his hut, the night-time

wailing over the dead;
        and then he throws the empty bottle
away, still stinking of rum,

the reeling truth
        rolled out into those streets.

6

When I look at that long photographic
      exposure of the Gaillard Cut

in the slow, myriad 1913 that was,
      I see a ship, a hull

scooped out of the earth – imagined in the digging.
      Railway tracks are laid meticulously

between Gold and Contractors Hills,
      locomotives, dirt trains, rock drills

strewn along the base of the canal,
      glimmers of mud here and there,

drenched clothes, but timid, far-off
      points of light glint like guardian ports;

and then at last the men put down their shovels
      and look up

and see mineral oils, copper, iron,
      molasses, canned foods,

lumber, coffee, wheat and coal
      passing serenely overhead.

7

Wherever they cut away the land
        it kept coming back, sucked in.

What did they hope to hold onto here?
        Dynamite, steam shovels,

the dead, the dying?
        Or the marrying, babies,

a bride's dress flaring
        in Culebra, her steady gaze.

And the sliding energy
        of the clay when rainwater

penetrated so the clay
        all but flew off the rock

burying men, shovel and pickaxe.
        This is how it was:

the hill wanted to run back
        into the canal-pit and replace

what was taken away,
        and the human wanted to join up

the two oceans with weeping
        and wailing.

THE PACIFIC COAST

Fierce as the sunrise is,
       the sunset is even more so –
              coming as it does after so much event,

our shouts and laughter, our games on deck.
       We are moving past entire countries now.
              I cannot hang this knowledge over my shoulder

like a school satchel, or walk away from it
       like geography homework.
              In Santiago we will stay in a German pensión

and eat our potato soup at the long table, heads bowed
       with the other polite guests.
              I am no longer a child but have served

the apprenticeship of childhood.
       I am eleven now and it tells on me –
              a moroseness that comes over me

                  without warning, every now and then.

SOLACE

That's what it was and that's what this is –
        water pulled to and fro, interior water.

The Grace Line archive in a library
        in Throggs Neck, New York;

shipping timetables, internet postcards
        of the boats in the fifties –

the colours a little too gaudy
        to be real, bleeding into each other –

the *Santa Rosa, Santa Barbara,*
        Santa Maria, Santa Isabel, Santa Margarita,

decks empty and awash.
        And here I am again, a young girl

on the verge of puberty, awake
        in my cabin, as we sail

throughout the pure, restorative dark.
        If I were a peninsula I would try

and fail to free myself of land,
        I would be riddled with rain,

and wrestle all night with roots and rocks,
        not knowing where I begin or end.

I would draw the water round me.
        I would take my longest winter

and commend it to my shortest summer,
        because I want no more dryness,

                I want no more inland.

LIKE IT IS

I shared a cabin with my sister.
       I can still see the dark
between us, pixelated,

and feel her anguish
       and sense of betrayal
to be taken away, so far from home

and for so long. She kept a diary
       close by her bed.
Along the coast of Perú,

and near Arica, the stench of guano
       reached our ship. We could stare
at those whitened rocks from the deck,

slap slap slap over the interminable nesting places.
       And yes, the sun passed over them
like the flat of a hand

and drew out a lingering smell.
       Write about the guano, my sister tells me.

COASTLINE

Whatever it is – rock, sand, asphalt –
    I would still know it today

        as a mother pores over her child
           when he is long grown.

Surprising mornings – those countries that raised me,
    irresolute, failing now – surfaces

        I could still mingle with and cling to –

a courage as I get close to shore
    and then, where the water is shallow at last,

        a bottomless sense of arrival and displacement.

APPROACHES TO CHILE

> *¿Cuál es la verdad? ¿El río*
> *que fluye y pasa*
> *donde el barco y el barquero*
> *son también ondas de agua?*
> *¿O este soñar del marino*
> *siempre con ribera y ancla?*

> Which is the truth?
> The river that flows and passes
> where the boat and boatman
> are also waves of water?
> Or this dream of the sailor
> always of a shore and anchor?

Antonio Machado

1

All along, it was there:
        mountains, the start of a day –

        dark blue and reminders
of long hours to come, the shadows of fish

      in shallow water,
          no two moments the same ever.

Even now when I try to make
      a whole picture of it, there are just

vortices, salt on my lips, mica
      on the mountain

and I must be content with this.

2

When I first saw
       the port of Buenaventura –

             papaya, sweat and mango,
      the nearest I could get – or the real

distance from me now, my poor understanding –

I turned round in the square
         the church emptying itself,

girls dressed for first communion
         on the steps, a little laughter,

some gifts, I turned round as if against myself.

Will it reach you – reading this – my sorrow?

3

Each time I think
      it's here, we're here –

this time we're in a garden
      in Antofagasta:

a low white house, sand-land,
       sand like furious talk

and nothing understood.
       It must be so hard to grow here!

It must be such hard work
       for that lank rose, and a dark patch

around its stem where
        some thirsty person has poured

a jug of water so that this
        leaf, and this one, can happen:

be alive, that is
        in a time of desert.

4

My father is waiting on the quay.
        On the road to Santiago

I roll the car window all the way down.
        The mountain is near me

but leaning back, and if I duck down
        I can see as far as the sky.

My face is almost against the mountain
        and we are running with it

though what is it? – poverty-stricken
        scrubland and sun.

Look it is catching up
        it tells me

                love where you are

I offer you what I don't have
        give up everything for this feeling.

THE ANDES

Whenever I stayed on that riding farm
only a few miles from Santiago

I would go for long walks alone
out into the almond orchard

that had so many points of entry and exit.
I would step over the horse manure in the pasture,

the weather would be fine and dry, good
for riding bareback.

As I walked I approached the Andes –
an intelligence, intricate as those fingerprints

on rocks in the Valle del Encanto
where figures were carved in stripes

and circles – head-dresses, staring eyes,
mouthless and faint in the sun.

I was 12, the Andes just ahead,
stepping back from me in a kind of easy,

lasting dance, an easy dare.

CLOTH

For now it's not that anymore:
>   not the detail of it – whether there really was

a hill behind Gabriel's house, or whether I wore
>   a crinoline that day, or walked down Vitacura

with my friend Monona, whatever ragged
>   scraps of memory I can be educated by

now, so many years later, or near-memories:
>   us girls standing in line for the movies

in Las Lilas wearing lipstick to look older.
>   But that like a fabric I can still

smooth over with my hand – I was there,
>   I breathed that air that riffled

where I was and occasionally took even the sea
>   by surprise, and I felt no more

than the strain of distance pulling
>   at the four corners of me

yet nothing gave.

GLASS TABLE

I stepped out on the patio.
The wind had given up its chase.
I sat down at the glass table.

My sister had been sent to relatives
in Spain – no one understood
why she was ill, starving,

or why she was so remote.
I lived out her absence
and I lived this country for her.

I wanted her home.
I began a long letter to her
and told her light, silly stories,

anecdotes she could enjoy,
so she would at least
feel my presence out there

where she wasn't with us,
and there would be nothing
to disturb her

in my careful connected writing
both sides of airmail paper
and she wouldn't see through me.

CORDILLERA

Away the clouds go, downriver.

    These are new lessons, sheer and unalterable,

a stone house someone loves,

        high orchards, a sensitivity,

the gravity of the distance home

      in the grip of a cold, fast river.

I learn how not to be afraid

        or alone among these mountains.

Here is what I must grow towards

      and here is the shadow I must live under.

PEDRO DE VALDIVIA

. . . Es la más abundante de pastos y sementeras, y para darse todo género de ganado y plantas que se puede pintar; mucha y muy linda madera para hacer casas . . .* Letter to the Emperor Carlos V, 4 September 1545

At last I come to the Plaza de Armas,
        a yellow and white town hall
and a statue of Valdivia on a horse.

A few stray hairs blow across his eyes.
        In the gritty, modern air
he opens a packet of sweets for me,

the reds and greens and yellows
        spill immoderately, and the wrapper
drags a little on past the palms.

He is the soul of courtesy
        to me, daughter of a Spaniard.
He is what he was – ambitious,

high above the glances of passers-by,
        the friends who agree to meet
'a los pies del caballo',

all those eager, terrified
        or gentle inhabitants with no horses.
His horse wades through sand, thirst,

sediment, strong currents, prevailing rains,
        down to the edible valley.
Its soft lips and yellow teeth reach for

the tough *quillay* leaves on the slopes,
        long sweet grasses that blow its way for a time.

*. . . *it is most abundant in pastures and sown fields, and good for raising every kind of livestock and plant you can describe; lots of very beautiful wood to build houses* . . .

quillay: soap bark tree

COD LIVER OIL

Of course I had to have it, a tablespoonful
and swallow it all at once, clear and yellow.

As when I step out from the raft onto the illicit pond
and my body knows what shivering is, shuddering,

but I pretend I can be like the water strider –
skid out over it forever.

How hopeless it is to argue about the sickly taste
of the rice in perfect white mounds, glutinous

in the school dining hall at Santiago College,
or not to feel fear at the illegible algebra on the blackboard.

The girlish orange trees line up in rows
in the school courtyards, where we wander after lunch

diluting it all, and then of course that ends too.
The trees have gathered round the pond

to see me enter. I can never throw off
my dread of such things, trials

I have to pass through –
before what? What my mother wanted for me

as she held the brimming spoon to my mouth –
to mean it, to be alive, tingling with life,

afterwards altering the taste of everything subtly.

DROPPED STITCHES

I start again, I start again.
The chill is going from my hands as I knit,
counting. I tug away the top rows carefully

to get rid of the last mistakes.
They float off somewhere historical
or hierarchical, these light, gone, telegraphic places

that I make with my own two hands:
what I give away, not knowing
how it happened, how I did it.

MOSAIC

One by one we lay down the tiny squares
        – funnels, a black hull, a name
on the stern – a few letters rubbed out.

We can manage these too: barnacles or lichen,
        whatever attaches and holds,
and here we lay the shadow of the Humboldt Current

so it can nourish the ocean, here whole countries
        we pass as if it were no big deal,
place, place and place – the dry mountains,

till we see a fleeting glaze over the mosaic
        like a fabulous wind over the Andes,
and then know where to stop.

How many years before you belong
        in a new country, before you want to
lie in its land when you die?

POPLARS

for Marisol Téllez,
remembering the refugees from the Spanish Civil War in Chile,

1

In those early days, what was there?
      At first there was a sun,

a small white house
      in a field, like something missing, or climbing

nowhere – a ladder for instance and no apple tree;
      sleep, *chirimoyas* close to the lips

but for someone else. Loose leaves
      blowing, a grating of earth-shoes

on the road, showing us the way,
      barriers higher than any mountains we knew

before we came here.
      Yes we saw it then, through half-shut eyes,

another earth, another manner of being,
      a child alone in a field, hungry,

and the worst over. And the poplars always
      persuasive and masking.

chirimoyas: custard apples

2

A little left-over sunlight
　　　　on a faraway plain

and on Zurbarán's silver dish
　　　　where a cup rests, or disturbs:

the water in that cream cup
　　　　is deeper and more imaginary

than any lake, certain, contained
　　　　and worked, open and salutary,

but going. A rose lying on the wide, flat rim
　　　　of the plate conveys itself too

as once it was, all its petals
　　　　peering outward, not destitute.

There is moisture in it still.
　　　　I give, give away this cup of water.

I mean for it not to alter,
　　　　or my thirst to go.

3

How painstakingly one reality
　　　　becomes another.

I think of everything that way, where we were,
　　　　how our boat made the distance work

so hard, like a call to prayer,
        the effort of raising the sky each morning

           laboriously laying it down again.

Then we came to the Equator
        and the sun rose continually

           in our minds, and taught us
to move away from each other

        as if away from too much hurt, too much heat.

A band of sun like a blindfold.

4

Children in the back of a pickup truck
        on their way to the French border:

their eyes flicker, their hands hold on tight.

Any reminder: for instance an occasional
        rush along the leaves, upward

or a faint, even restorative
        hiatus when the breeze loses its force . . .

My own child sees the poplars now.
        He finds a dry riverbed
           along the border of a field.

He runs towards them.

5

Whenever I walk in the country they always
　　　entreat me to stand still,
　　　　　or grope for something –

　　　　　　omissions and certainties.

The relief when I think of them, here,
　　　　　or far away in my own country.

In their turbulence
　　　　　is a feeling of thirst gone.

　　　As I finish my sentence
the field darkens

　　　and the poplars darken in their own lost time.

MANJAR

It seems so mysterious that I could really
        have lived in that valley all those years ago
doing who knows what so earnestly and busily,

alive, alive by the Mapocho, or under the almond trees
        making sure of me (now you see her)
yet all along with nothing very memorable happening,

just the present-continuous with its endless
        stops and sticky starts, anxieties that store up,
the present imperfect with its soft familial

inconsistency, the second-person familiar
        each time more familiar, *tú y tú*, more fluent.
And the boiled, sweet, yellowy condensed milk

on my breakfast bread that also spreads
        into my consciousness today
in such an ephemeral and enduring way

as I waited to eat it, as I held out my hand for it.

manjar: caramel spread

ACCENTS

I lay down under the cherry trees
in our garden, where the grass was balding

a little, and looked up into the branches.
I was learning the catechism,

and I went over a few questions
and answers as absolutes; I was thinking

of a dance I had been to on a farm,
a dress I wore, something I said

too revealing of feeling;
those chicks left in an open crate

in the shade behind the farm, near a wall,
came into my mind. I thought of how

they might have struggled all wet
out of their eggs, like light escaping;

Señorita Morales came into my thoughts too,
her long fingernails when she pointed out

where the accents should go over the words
on the blackboard, and the way she said

penúltima sílaba, and *antepenúltima;*
and all these thoughts lightly hooked together

like young girls walking down the street
holding each others' hands by the little finger.

TO CHILE

For some time now I have left
        absolutely unbroken a line of thought

to bring you back to me –
        pack-mules climbing or resting

in the mountains,
        that know the paces between

these pines and acacias,
        leading down to open country –

only a brief measure
        between mountain and sea.

I see dead seals washed up
        on a shore near La Serena,

light that softens and then vanishes,
        assignments I set myself and accomplish

so that slowly, knot by knot,
        I pull myself closer to you –

my illimitable plan to speak of you.
        Those poplars along a field –

I tremble for them, and I invite you, elegiac seal,
        to a hospitable depth.

ESPINOS

We leave the coast for the intense
summer evenings of Santiago –

gardens stained dark with sprinklers,
the collective sigh of a crowd

entering a bus as one,
a maid in a blue-and-white checked

uniform, near some oleanders
deep in her own thoughts,

turning back indoors,
the mountains always up there

that seem sympathetic, or bereft – tempting,
whatever you want them to be.

The *espinos* on the foothills we pass
ask so little, so little water and fuss:

anxiety and affliction, solace,
seem to take place in another dimension.

It takes so long for night to fall here
among their tiny leaves, the *quirincas* –

brown seed-pods that waver,
thorny twigs the sun still basks in.

espinos: acacia caven, native to Chile

ARAUCARIA ARAUCANA

In my notebook the pages
tumble over the spirals

easily. I work at each morose
breeze, each arduous stillness.

There are times when I mean
only avoidance and resolution,

resistance, when you were looking
for shelter, the taking up of stones

to defend you. But I can offer
brilliance, a blue-green

composure that hardly sways.
Isn't that enough?

In the meditative night
aren't my limitations reassuring

though the presence of the sky
is never hidden, or kind?

araucaria araucana: monkey-puzzle tree, native to Chile

INVISIBLE INK

for Sofía Prats

CHIRIMOYA

Now, what was it you said?
Was it about suffering?

Each black shiny pip I hold
in my mouth – and what is gone now.

I slice the *chirimoya* and pour
orange juice over it – even over

the holes torn where the pips were.
Must I take these children by the hand

who are all holding hands
and open out like paper dolls?

Or the communion that melts instantly
on my tongue in another life?

I drink from the river of typhoid.
A poplar makes itself out before sunrise,

then there is a mesh of bees restoring the air
just where the cool horizon is.

Is, isn't. Across the dark somehow
I can leap over my own sadness, or someone else's.

Orange, pink and red are the votive candles
in the marketplace, heaven-held.

chirimoya: custard apple

SANTIAGO

It's what you're used to
       and can't do without now:

a line of mountains wherever you go,
       as you enter each street

a chance to think with a higher curiosity
       and give way to whatever is immoveable

and offers grace or direction –
       a family, a cause – or these Andes,

so you always know where you are,
       you are always in relation to them,

close as the red shop where you go to buy milk,
       or when you talk and they are there

in the corner of your eye,
       as if hanging on your words.

What I live with day after day
       though I am deep in the city, or lost

and they are like so many days
       that happen immeasurably,
              in which I fear not.

CALLAMPAS

Cross the avenue from our house
and there are the huts – wooden slats,

cardboard, tar, anything to hand
held loosely together in an empty lot

and the habitual love of the sunrise
travelling so far to meet them

but then obliterating them
so we see them at first

and then don't see or want to
in the glare

or we forget to improvise a
roof over our eyes

with our hands, where our fingertips meet.

callampas: shanties

THE RICH

Now I see I did not go far enough,
    I did not go deep enough,

the place was wasted on me.
    I raced past everything, the baker's window,

the cookie crescents in floury sugar,
    the carpenter on the corner

who achieved so much those early mornings,
    wood-shavings already in little piles at his feet,

and even the mysterious gardens
    of the rich down Cristóbal Colón,

a father in the driveway with slicked-down hair,
    a mother in a lavender dress and high heels,

a child in a green and white checked uniform
    and straw hat.

THEIR GARDENS

I must speak again about the gardens
and see them as they were.

I looked so closely into them
on my way to school, as into another reality.

At one and the same time they were there as
porticoes, grass, protective cherry and almond trees,

swimming pools – deep gardens always
of intense, unbounded happiness

that broke up and re-gathered
in their own shadows;

and then they were also gardens
of the imagination

for those who would never have them,
with the sense of a city pressing in –

impending and all-knowing;
places I could only see a little bit

into from the road, grape arbours, soft conversations,
a maid and a gardener who lived

in a narrow room behind the kitchen, with their little girl.
And she had two long braids.

STREET, SANTIAGO 1973

When did it begin?

Two sides of the same street
       tear away from each other,

delaying: the communality
       of street. And before you know it,

(and it is quick now, after such gradual
       preparations)

his eye is already pierced,
       her mouth broken, and this long before

any cry is heard, or a din
       becomes a headline, or a football

stadium a massacre, or those long hands
       at rest in a woman's lap

are wrung.

SOLDIER

It brushes past you at first in San Miguel –
    a decayed building,

a poster torn off, some letters remaining,
    a *p*, an *x* , is that an *o*?

each one trying to retrieve a complete thought:
    a soothing dream or idea you might say

like the reassuring blue paint dripped down
    a wooden restaurant on a fine day,

all the letters there: *papas fritas, pollo asado*,
    warmth inside, a table for you.

But then the concrete side of a stadium
    looms up where you did things

and saw things you don't want to say
    or spell out (today, on an outing

with your grandchildren
    picking apples in an orchard,

and Luisito leaps over the shade
    into raw sunlight

where some apples have rolled,
    how beautiful he is).

THE DISAPPEARED

In invisible ink their trajectory
seems to show only at

selected moments in the day, moments
of toy UV light, guards down,

a faultline; here we can just see
a point of departure

which is also the place
where they did not say goodbye,

and a point of arrival
when mothers cannot embrace

their children again
the ones who grew up

and were disappeared.
But the moments are not really

deleted, or jumping like
mountain goats, crag

to crag. No, they drip,
they shine, they are revealed

from time to time, for anyone who wants to see.

TOCONAO

There must be a church here –
        because if I walk on these plates
                of dry mud, the earth tearing itself

apart – 'No way back' it says to me, or 'never leave' –
        all the things places say to you
                when you first arrive –

or 'there is nothing here for you'.
        Those erased mountains along the horizon,
                erased and erased, till there is no more

                        to erase to the left, and to the right
only a glimmer of what they were, but going fast.
        A white stone bell-tower. My child in a blue

                and white checked shirt, yellow shorts,
turning with his arms held out.

We are wherever the early morning
        sun finds us, helpless, and restores us.

VOLCÁN VILLARRICA

Someone must still live here:
     collapsing planks of wood,
          stakes in the ground,

a shed, a claim, barbed wire,
     tall dry grey grass in a season of plenty.

Roundabout the house are sheepfolds,
     fresh, interior trees,
          roof that sags for years into the earth,

jagged stick-like shadows
     wavering, a heady heat
          as if someone were weeping

or wept here once and left.
     The volcano behind the house
          is covered with snow, a bereavement of snow,

and the force all around the volcano
     is imponderable, immovable and kind, patient.

RETURNING

A field comes to me,
        a wedge of wind

                puma in the woods
                        and the woods impenetrable

like closed eyelids.

            I remember a gate, part of a hill,
                and that I couldn't go on,

a wrong turning leading to
        a sheepskin hanging across a barn door

                the cry of a rooster
before I was really awake,

and an apple orchard,
        entangled branches low to the ground.

The orchards, the orchards, the orchards!

            The ones you enter on your hands
                        and knees.

APPLE ORCHARD

I step into one shadow
        that is the meaning of one tree,

each shadow the receding
        thoughts of a tree;

or still, a thumbprint
        or contusion of a tree,

true to it, run-away
        with its spirit,

like the worn-out shirt
        of a father or son

she may hold to her face
        among the jagged

patches of sunlight
        left free, and delineated

freely, as if at random,
        by all the joined shadows.

FIESTAS PATRIAS

The shanties try hard to stay awake
    in the penumbra.

How can it be so dark so early
    yet warm, or so moving

to those who see it – the crests
    of the hills,

a last light on wood planks
    or mud, tar,

long grass headed for a road up there?
    And they keep on opening their doors

so we can see how they live –
    as if creeks, forgotten rivers

were exposed to an aerial view
    where the farming of lines starts:

a continuity – handkerchiefs flickering,
    a couple, a blind accordionist on his horse

    leaning back, lost in a song.

fiestas patrias: independence day celebrations

TUNA

My feet entering this mountain river
                    go white and numb.
        I wear the white socks of numbness.

        They are like an event.
When I reach for the cactus fruit – *tuna,*
                    it releases tiny hair-like thorns
        into the palm of my hand.

I search for them now. Sometimes
        I hold my hand up
                    to the pale blue sky to find them.

I open the ochre of the *tuna* and I am alive,
        its seeds run through me.

Now my arms in the river are numb, my body
        like those Aymara weavings, the dyes circulating
                    then stilled, all those feelings I will ever feel

mapped out. What is happening to my feet, my hands?
                    My feet and my hands can just touch
                        the two ends of Chile –

I lie north to south in it, I am as slim
        as good fortune, as the man who has walked
                    all the way here, over the mountains.

I meet its fleeting rigour
        with numbness and a variable pain.

tuna: prickly pear

COLIHUACHOS

They find me out, glistening,
   burnished, rising and lowering
suddenly above the high rage

of the river Saltos del Petrohué
   but then persistently come near me –
the volcano in the corner of my eye –

and adhere to the sweat of my arm
   with its sweet sweet smell of hardship, road,
heat, laughter, an unrest,

or hover higher than me or the spray or foam –
   up where the world begins,

then alight and would stay.

colihuachos: horseflies

LAGO TODOS LOS SANTOS

A long way to get here,
a narrow way –
my shoulders are drawn in
to pass through the time
and thought it takes.

I put my palms down on the water
as if it were a desk I can learn on.
My boy picks up the black and red
volcanic stones. He plays on the slopes.

The volcano makes playthings for him.
Each stone has its own unfathomable
past, my own failures light and porous.

*

Who did I know? Who knew me?
Each new place I smooth with my hand
is a domesticated circle I have to leave.
High slopes, overhanging branches.

And there is still the remaining, unsaid
far end of the lake.
A boast that we can do it –
go way out, past what we see now,
in our red and yellow boat.

The mountains drift,
and the water is turquoise.
The volcano is always nearby
though we travel and travel away from it.
It's not too late, we can stay a little longer.
My boy sleeps on my shoulder.

TO MY SON ASLEEP

I see you now asleep,
your eyes partly open still –

so that, partially, light spills out, in
entering leanly, a lean-to.

There is compromise in it,
a weather-eye, or a place

only half believed in, dream
or reality. But you, you –

my child, illusion of my days,
finer than those Andes

I used to see from my bedroom window
in Santiago, sleep well,

while sky and land break through
like good or bad news,

one after the other, comforting or yawning dark,
a patchwork of human error unfolded

in a very precise curve of light
to mark your place in the world, senses,

wakefulness and the mystery of sleep
one and the same –

you see it all as light pours in and passes.

NÍSPERO
for Redha and Ramy

The road also curls up
like the sole of an old shoe

but ends here at the back of a low house
or on and on (not ending –
the road going into the house)

past the garden, lavender,
lemon and loquats - *nísperos,*
eucalyptus, olive trees bent double

preventing any sun from entering
(or stealthily only), the most beautiful
and luxuriant shade, smooth

like the brown shiny pips of the *níspero.*
The scorched leaves curl
and fail, but the yellow fruit is fine

and essential. I rub the *níspero* against my sleeve
to take off the fuzz
because, listen – what I wanted

was not the city, or a road to a high mountain
but this path to a small house
where I have to make my way

and it is almost too dark to see
among the struggling trees
and fruit as given to me.

COCHAYUYO

How many times I discovered it,
            leaking iodine, fallen into its own arms

along the coast, black-brown, tubular
            with orange-red tinges

or pale green new ribbons
            lifting just above the current.

It is knit with such longing,
            this gravitational shawl that may

or may not be land, and says to me
            'homestead', 'integral';

when I wanted to believe all along
            it could end somewhere – in some shop

at the back of my mind
            where dry seaweed is hung in sunlight

or overflows in baskets.
            And now that I've seen it again,

how can I live without it,
            clogging, hiding everywhere I knew once,

or go away when staying is so fluent,
            going or staying so abundant, restless?

cochayuyo: edible seaweed

THE ROOM AND THE ROAD

River I cannot swim from
           rinses those reeds, the whistling
                high moments of reeds

so I can understand what it is to travel,
           endure, slip lightly
                from one country to another

as if I were pulling off shirts,
           like the approach to the beige
                and pink church in Andacollo

after struggling for days through cactus land,
           a church that is all light,
                no shadow sees it yet;

then I enter the crypt
           and I can just make out
                jewels, badges, crutches

left behind to thank the Virgin
           for saving a life, for making good;
                so quiet and unexceptional

must this reverie be at first,
           this casting off
              of all I own –

even the sturdiest ground,
           where a tree shakes itself free in the rain
                and the room knows.